NATIONAL GEOGRAPHIC

D0100737

From the Skyscraper

Marvin Buckley

From the skyscraper
I can see streets.

HAPPY HILLS BALLROOM
JVT DISCOUNT CENTER
PERFUMES COSMETICS TOILETRIES SUNGLASSES
DISCOUNT CENTER
HISPANO AMERICANA DE CAMBIO LTD.
Dominican $ Express
HARDWARE
HOUSEWARES
GIFTWARES
PIZZA TOPE

3

People drive on the streets.

From the skyscraper
I can see office buildings.

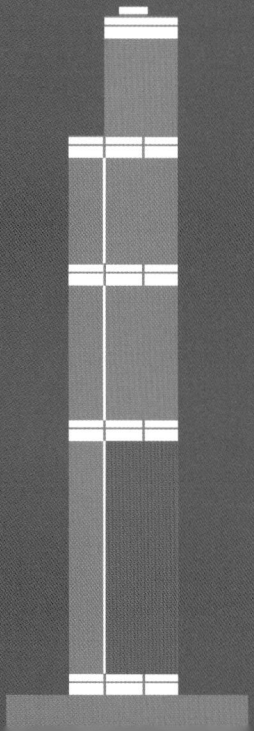

EXECUTIVE PLA

People work in
the office buildings.

From the skyscraper
I can see a park.

People jog in the park.

From the skyscraper
I can see a lake.

People sail boats
on the lake.

C
22
12156

From the skyscraper
I can see an airport.

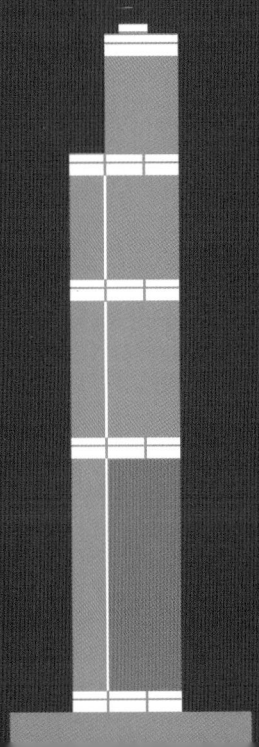

People get on planes at the airport.

B43
6673

From the skyscraper
I can see a baseball field.

People enjoy the big game.